INVESTIGATING
MYSTERIOUS
PLACES

MACHU PICCHU

LOST CITY OF THE INCAS

by Scott Sonneborn

CAPSTONE PRESS
a capstone imprint

Published by Capstone Press, an imprint of Capstone
1710 Roe Crest Drive, North Mankato, Minnesota 56003
capstonepub.com

Copyright © 2025 by Capstone. All rights reserved. No part of this publication may be reproduced in whole or in part, or stored in a retrieval system, or transmitted in any form or by any means, electronic, mechanical, photocopying, recording, or otherwise, without written permission of the publisher.

Library of Congress Cataloging-in-Publication Data is available on the Library of Congress website.

ISBN: 9781669093497 (hardcover)
ISBN: 9781669093442 (paperback)
ISBN: 9781669093459 (ebook PDF)

Summary: Climb high into the Andes Mountains of Peru to discover Machu Picchu, the hidden city built by the Inca Empire. How did the Inca people build such an amazing city with huge stones, and why was it abandoned? This book is your guide to one of the world's most mysterious ancient cities.

Editorial Credits
Editor: Donald Lemke; Designer: Tracy Davies; Media Researcher: Svetlana Zhurkin; Production Specialist: Katy LaVigne

Image Credits
Alamy: Lordprice Collection, 18, Prisma Archivo, 17, Science History Images, 27, Ville Palonen, 23; Bridgeman Images: © Look and Learn, 13, Future Publishing Ltd, 6; Dreamstime: Cosmopol, 22, Jesse Kraft, 25; Getty Images: Anh Vo, 19, Fotosearch, 20; Newscom: Danita Delimont Photography/Peter Langer, 21; Shutterstock: AKalenskyi (Machu Picchu icon), cover and throughout, Aleksandar Todorovic, 14, Aliaksei Hintau (smoke background), 2 and throughout, Angela Meier, 15, clairemphotography, cover, Erich Schultz, 5, Everton Lourenco, 26, Jerome Stubbs, 7, Leo McGilly, 10, pablopicasso, 29, Peter Hermes Furian, 9, Rafael Martin-Gaitero, 12, Uwe Bergwitz, 11

Any additional websites and resources referenced in this book are not maintained, authorized, or sponsored by Capstone. All product and company names are trademarks™ or registered® trademarks of their respective holders.

TABLE OF CONTENTS

Chapter One
CITY IN THE CLOUDS..4

Chapter Two
BUILDING AN EMPIRE...8

Chapter Three
LOST AND FOUND...16

Chapter Four
MYSTERIES REMAIN..20

GLOSSARY..30
READ MORE..31
INTERNET SITES...31
INDEX..32
ABOUT THE AUTHOR...32

Chapter One

CITY IN THE CLOUDS

Machu Picchu is a very **mysterious** place. This **ancient** city sits atop a tall mountain in South America.

Machu Picchu hides among the clouds. It is hard to see from lower down on the mountain. Getting to the city can be difficult too!

Machu Picchu is a very old place. A group of people called the Incas built the stone city more than 500 years ago. Experts still have many questions about the city.

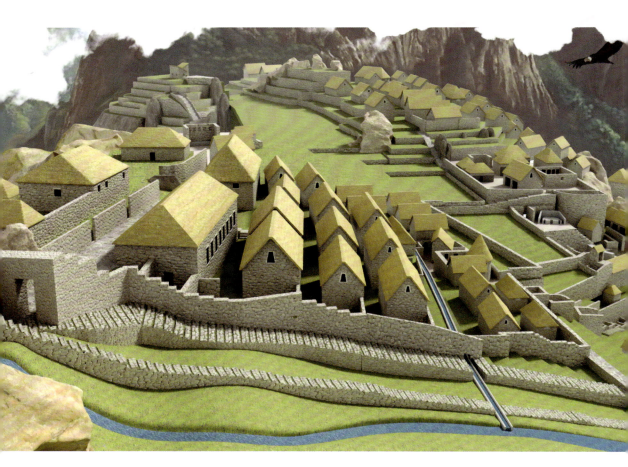

An illustration of Machu Picchu in the mid-1400s

How did the Inca people build a city in such a high-up place? Why did they build it? Was the city a royal palace or a prison? No one knows for sure.

 FACT

In 1983, Machu Picchu became a World Heritage Site to honor and protect its history.

Chapter Two

BUILDING AN EMPIRE

The Inca **civilization** began in what is now the country of Peru. Starting in 1438, the Inca people took over a large part of South America.

Within just a few years, their **empire** covered more than 350,000 square miles (906,000 square kilometers). It was the largest empire on Earth at the time!

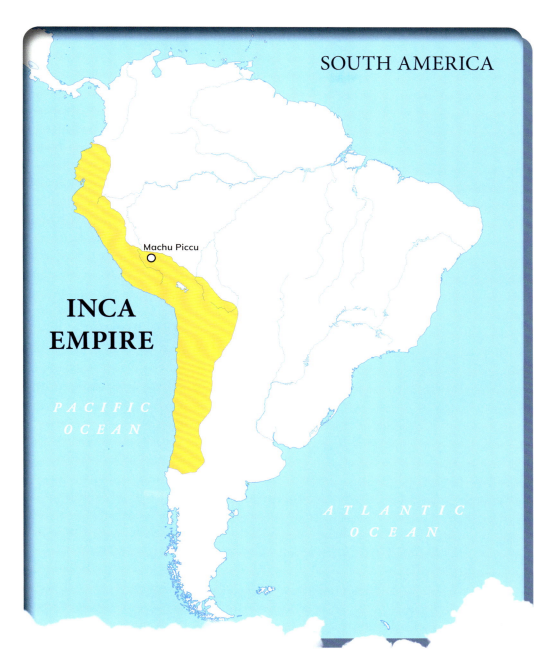

The Inca Empire during the early 1500s

The city of Aguas Calientes sits in the valley below Machu Picchu.

The Inca people built Machu Picchu on the peak of a mountain that's 8,000 feet (2,400 meters) tall. Machu Picchu means "old peak" in their language.

The Inca people didn't have horses or wheels. So how did they move giant stones up a mountain? It sounds almost impossible!

Large stones frame an ancient doorway in Machu Picchu.

Archaeologists know the Inca people were great builders who were up to the task. In fact, they built more than 12,000 miles (19,000 kilometers) of roads across their empire.

This fortress in Peru shows the incredible skills of Inca builders.

Inca communities had many builders and craftspeople.

Many experts believe the Inca people used logs to roll boulders up the mountain. Then they used smaller stones and bronze tools to carve the boulders into building blocks.

Most of the blocks were carved from a hard stone called **granite**. Some of the blocks weigh more than 55 tons (50 metric tons)!

Giant blocks fit together like a puzzle.

Despite their size, the blocks fit together perfectly. After hundreds of years and many earthquakes, the buildings still stand just as they did when they were built.

Chapter Three

LOST AND FOUND

In 1532, an army from Spain **conquered** the Inca Empire. They destroyed many Inca cities and **temples**.

The Spanish never found the hidden city of Machu Picchu. Hardly anyone knew about the city for 400 years.

Francisco Pizarro led the Spanish invasion of Peru.

In 1911, an American professor named Hiram Bingham traveled to Peru. He wanted to learn more about the Inca people. Guided by a local man named Melchor Arteaga, Bingham rediscovered Machu Picchu.

Hiram Bingham during an expedition in 1912

When the professor got back to the United States, he told of his findings. The City in the Clouds became famous. Today, nearly two million people visit Machu Picchu every year!

Chapter Four

MYSTERIES REMAIN

The Inca people did not write things down on paper. Instead of writing, they tied knots in string. These knotted strings were called **quipus**.

An Inca holding quipus used for recording information

The knotted strings could hold answers to many Machu Picchu mysteries. But no one knows how to read the quipus.

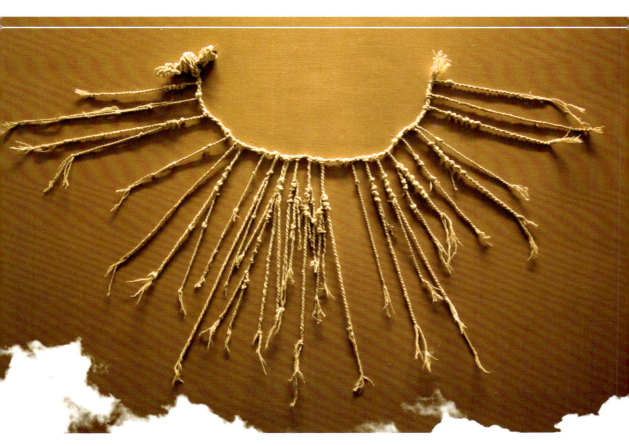

Inca quipus at a Peruvian museum

Experts disagree about why the Inca people built Machu Picchu. Some think Inca rulers took vacations at the mountaintop city.

The royal palace in Machu Picchu

The Inca king's toilet in Machu Picchu

Why do they think that? Archaeologists have discovered a palace in Machu Picchu. This palace even has a private bath with its own toilet!

Some experts believe Machu Picchu was an important place in the Inca religion. There are many special temples there.

The Temple of the Sun is at the very top of Machu Picchu. It was designed so that the sun shines straight through its windows on the longest day of the year.

FACT

Machu Picchu is one of the "New Seven Wonders of the World," a list of unbelievable, human-made places around the globe.

Other historians have studied these temples and think that Machu Picchu was actually a giant calendar. The way the sun hit certain buildings on different days told the Inca when to plant their crops.

Inca people may have used the Intihuatana stone at Machu Picchu like a calendar.

Inca people planting seeds in spring

There are also historians and archaeologists who think that Machu Picchu was all of these things!

Why it was built may be one of the mysteries of Machu Picchu we never solve.

Glossary

ancient (AYN-shent)—very old; something that happened a long, long time ago

archaeologist (ar-kee-OL-uh-jist)—a scientist who digs up and studies old things left by people from the past

conquer (KAHN-ker)—to defeat or gain control by force

civilization (sih-vihl-luh-ZAY-shuhn)—a group of people with their own languages and way of life

empire (EM-pyre)—a big area of many places controlled by one ruler or government

granite (GRAN-it)—a very hard rock; it's what some kitchen counters are made of

mysterious (mis-TEER-ee-us)—when something is very hard to understand or figure out, like a secret puzzle

quipu (KEE-poo)—a special way the Inca people recorded events not with pen and paper, but by tying knots in strings

temple (TEM-pul)—a special building where people go to worship or show respect for what they believe in

Read More

Golkar, Golriz. *Science of Machu Picchu.* North Mankato, MN: Capstone, 2022.

Stine, Megan. *Where Is Machu Picchu?* New York: Penguin Workshop, 2018.

Weitzman, Elizabeth. *Mysteries of Machu Picchu.* Minneapolis: Lerner Publishing Group, Inc., 2018.

Internet Sites

National Geographic: Discover 10 Secrets of Machu Picchu
nationalgeographic.com/travel/article/secrets

Peru: Attraction: Machu Picchu
peru.travel/en/attractions/machu-picchu

UNESCO: World Heritage Convention: Historic Sanctuary of Machu Picchu
whc.unesco.org/en/list/274

Index

archaeologists, 12, 23, 28
Arteaga, Melchor, 18

Bingham, Hiram, 18–19

calendar, 26

empire, 8, 12, 16

granite, 14

Inca Empire, 8, 12, 16
Inca people, 6, 7, 8, 11, 12, 13, 18, 20, 22

mountain, 4, 10, 11, 13, 22

Peru, 8, 12, 17, 18

quipus, 20–21

religion, 24
roads, 12
rulers, 22

South America, 4, 8
Spanish, 16, 17
stones, 6, 11, 13

Temple of the Sun, 24
tourism, 19

About the Author

Scott Sonneborn is the author of more than 40 books for kids. He's also written a bunch of TV shows and been nominated for both an Emmy and a Hugo Award. He lives in Los Angeles with his wife and their two sons.